I0101644

The I Know Everything About Everything Phenomenon

THE I KNOW EVERYTHING ABOUT EVERYTHING PHENOMENON

HOW SUCCESS IN BUSINESS OR PROFESSIONS CAN CREATE PROBLEMS AND WHAT TO DO ABOUT THEM

Douglas Soat

All rights reserved.
No part of this book may be reproduced in any form without written permission from
the publisher:
2017 Douglas Soat
dms@soatcp.com
ISBN: 0998868116
ISBN 13: 9780998868110

ACKNOWLEDGEMENTS

I want to thank my family, especially my wife, Lynn, for their support while I was writing this book.

I want to express gratitude to my son, John, for his design of the book's cover.

Finally, I want to thank Mrs. Melissa Van Tassell for her hard work in typing the manuscript.

Doug Soat, Ph.D.

TABLE OF CONTENTS

DEDICATION

This book is dedicated to the many fine CEO's, other executives, physicians, attorneys, professors and other professionals whom I have met, known, worked with, and heard about. You have done great things and have helped countless people live better lives.

This book was not written to bash all successful people. It was, however, written to identify a scourge in our society that serves to hurt your good names: the pompous, know-it-alls who believe they are God's gifts to society. Many of them are so hopelessly arrogant that they won't see themselves in the forthcoming pages, but the people whom they have hurt and whose lives they have tarnished or ruined will surely recognize them.

It is my sincere hope that at least a few of these unfortunate souls will, with the help of others who care about them and some qualified outside professionals, at least attempt to minimize some of their harmful behavior. Fortunately, I believe it is possible to do so.

Douglas M. Soat, Ph.D.

INTRODUCTION

Successful people are all around us: CEO's, other executives, physicians, lawyers, psychologists, dentists, engineers, etc. One of the traits shared by most successful people is self-confidence. It's important; we want our neurosurgeon to be confident before she does our brain surgery.

However, what happens to some successful people is that their self-confidence erodes into extreme arrogance. They start to believe they can do no wrong and they know everything there is to know about their area of expertise. That's bad enough, but eventually they begin to believe that they're experts in every field: politics, religion, and every other facet of life.

That's when they start to cause problems for themselves and everyone around them. That is when they succumb to The I Know Everything About Everything Phenomenon, which I will refer to as "The Phenomenon" (TP). Who are these people and what can be done about it? I will explore these issues in this book.

The people discussed are all real, not fictional. The anecdotes, some of which may seem hard to believe, are all true. The individuals discussed in this book are nearly all anonymous. To guarantee their anonymity, fictitious names are used and some facts have been changed. The purpose of this book is not to embarrass anyone. Instead, the goal is to identify people who have succumbed to what I refer to as "The Phenomenon". I have provided a sample test later in this book, which people can use to see whether they exhibit TP. Unfortunately, since many people find it difficult to see themselves as others do, it's probably more accurate and helpful to have someone who knows the individual well and is willing to be candid to take the test regarding the person in question.

If someone does succumb to The Phenomenon, what can be done about it? I'll provide suggestions later in this book to help people and those around them to identify approaches to minimize this malady.

I have worked as a Consulting Psychologist in business for over twenty-five years so far and I worked as a human resources executive for eighteen years prior to that. In that time, I've met and worked with many CEO's and other executives. I have also encountered many physicians, attorneys, engineers, dentists, and numerous other people. Most of those people have been very successful in their respective fields of endeavor. Unfortunately, some of them have become victims of their own success; they now believe they know everything about medicine, law, engineering, etc. Some of them even believe that they are experts in all facets of life and they are not bashful about showing off their alleged expertise to everyone they meet. Those are the people I will talk about in this book.

CHAPTER 1

WHAT IS THE I KNOW EVERYTHING ABOUT EVERYTHING PHENOMENON?

As a business psychologist, I have done in-depth assessments of several thousand executives, managers, sales people, engineers, and others. I use an in-depth interview of two to two-and-a-half hours, plus some tests: one on critical thinking, one on leadership style, and two personality inventories. Based on that, I develop a five to fifteen page report on the person which outlines the person's strengths, developmental needs, potential and recommendations regarding hiring. I try to assess how well the person matches the job, the supervisor, and the corporate culture.

Because of this, I believe I am an expert in employee selection. However, I don't know all there is to know about selecting people. I still learn things every day to get better at it. Unfortunately, some of the people I have assessed, met, worked with, and known about, don't see a need to keep learning. They think they already know all there is to know about their area of expertise. Few people would admit this, of course, but it becomes obvious after you talk to them for a while.

Working with someone who exhibits characteristics of The Phenomenon can be extremely frustrating. Obviously, they don't need to get advice from others because they already have all the answers.

One person I worked with said something once that suggested he might have exhibited TP. I explained why I did not recommend a particular person for a job and he said, "I respect your opinion. I just respect mine a lot more."

He ended up hiring the executive anyway, despite my recommendation not to do so. The person ended up to be a failure in the job and was later fired. Unfortunately, the man who made the above statement didn't follow some of my other hiring recommendations either and the organization suffered because of it (i.e., they lost a lot of money and had a number of significant problems they would not have had if they had followed my recommendations).

A person who succumbs to TP not only thinks that she knows everything about her area of expertise, she also does not admit her mistakes or finds some convenient excuse for what happened.

A person whom I worked with refused to admit his mistakes. The industrial equipment company that employed him had experienced production employees who were complaining that new people made the same wage that they did. They obviously wanted to make more money than new hires. However, this man said, "We need to reduce the wages of new people so that our experienced people don't complain." When the head of HR pointed out that new hires were already making barely above the minimum wage, which resulted in extreme difficulty in hiring good people, he said, "Well we can't afford to increase the pay of our experienced people, so we will now start paying new people the minimum wage. " He did not see the obvious logic in needing to pay experienced people more and leaving the wage of entry people the same (if not raising it).

This man had a financial background, not one in human resources. However, he believed he knew more than the head of HR about employee compensation. The head of the organization agreed with this person that the company could not afford to pay experienced people more money, so he implemented the action. When it became even harder to recruit good, new production people, the man who suggested cutting their wage still refused to admit that his idea was a poor one.

The person referred to above didn't admit his mistakes and he also exhibited another characteristic of people who succumb to TP: he didn't listen to advice from a person who knew more about the problem area than he did. The same was true about the man I referred to earlier who didn't accept my recommendation about not hiring a person.

Another example of a person who did not listen to others' advice because of symptoms of The Phenomenon was an executive from a sporting goods manufacturer. He refused to pay the commission to a recruiter who found a manager whom his firm hired. The executive refused to pay the fee because someone in his firm already knew the manager who was hired and told that to the executive. The executive, whom we'll call William, stated that he shouldn't have to pay the fee because the manager was already a known quantity. The recruiter stated, "I don't care if the manager is somebody's brother, if I gave you his name, you owe me the fee!"

The head of HR told William that the recruiter was correct, and even though it didn't seem fair since another employee already knew the man who was hired, they needed to pay the recruiter's fee nonetheless, according to the common practice in the recruiting industry as well as legal requirements.

William insisted that he wouldn't pay and didn't. The case was taken to court, William lost and he ended up paying more than the actual fee. Of course, he didn't admit that he should have listened to the head of HR because William was someone who exhibited numerous symptoms of The Phenomenon. He would not listen to sound advice from someone who knew what he was talking about and was much more qualified to give an opinion than William.

Another characteristic of those who suffer from TP is that they feel they are "special" and the rules and laws that apply to others don't apply to them.

An example of this was taken from one of my client companies. The CEO of this firm, a software design company, interviewed a candidate for a regional manager who was recommended by an executive recruiter. The CEO, whom we'll call Alan, interviewed the candidate. Since I also interviewed the person, Alan confided in me that he had asked the candidate, who had eight children, whether he was Catholic. I told Alan that was not an appropriate thing to ask him and that he could face some serious legal problems if the candidate ever complained to the EEOC. Alan said, "I know you're not supposed to ask that question, but it's okay, I can do that." Talk about hubris! He felt that the rules that apply to everyone else didn't apply to Alan because he was "special".

Some examples from the upper levels of government regarding people who feel the rules don't apply to them because they're "special" come to mind. But I won't go into that here, because this book is apolitical.

An additional facet of those who succumb to The Phenomenon is not demonstrating concern for employees. In my many years as a business psychologist, I have found that there are two necessary, but not sufficient, criteria for any successful supervisor, manager or executive: 1) setting high expectations for oneself and others; and 2) showing genuine concern for staff members' welfare.

The CEO of a company in the medical equipment industry, whom I'll call Patrick, had a corporate jet at his disposal. He wanted to use the jet, a very expensive Gulfstream model, for his own use because he was, after all "special" and didn't want to fly commercial and have to go through typical airports like "the peons". When he found out that if he were the only one to use the plane, he would have to declare it as income to the IRS, he decided that others would be able to use it, too. However, anyone who flew with him had to play by his rules. His rules indicated that everyone had to be "on time" so that the plane could take off when he wanted. His definition of "on time", however, was thirty minutes early.

So one day, when the plane was scheduled to depart from the local airport at 6:30 am, Patrick arrived at 6:10 a.m. After pacing back and forth for ten minutes because one person scheduled to be on the flight was not there yet, he declared, "That's it. I'm not waiting any more. We're leaving."

So the plane left at 6:20 am that morning. The unfortunate absent employee, who apparently didn't know that 6:30 a.m. on the schedule really meant "no later than 6:00 a.m." because the CEO was aboard, didn't get to fly on the corporate jet that day. I'm sure he learned a valuable lesson. I never found out whether he showed up at 6:25 with a shocked look on his face.

Patrick clearly didn't demonstrate a genuine concern for employees in this case because he wanted to leave when he was ready, not when the flight was scheduled or when everyone was there. Patrick was "special" so the rules of common courtesy didn't apply to him.

Related to the characteristic of feeling "special" is that of feeling "better" than everyone else. In the above example, Patrick didn't have a problem with leaving early because he felt he was "better" than the others scheduled to be on the jet. The others weren't CEO's, they weren't wealthy, and they didn't have a corner executive office. Patrick felt he was "better" than the others, so when he wanted to leave at 6:20, he saw no problem with telling the pilot of the jet to do so.

Another example of feeling "better" than others is when Patrick chose to build a new office. Calling it an office was almost a misnomer. It was more like an additional wing on the building. It was substantially bigger than any other office in the company. It had a fireplace, conference table, bar, sitting area, and desk. The room was so large I didn't even notice the desk the first time I saw the office, and the desk was not a small one. Patrick felt he deserved the over-sized office because he was "better" than others in the organization.

Getting back to my point about not showing genuine concern for employees' welfare as a characteristic of those succumbing to TP, I have another example of this.

Jackson was the President of a company in the petroleum industry. He, like Patrick, felt that he was "special" and "better" than others, so he, too, had a corporate jet at his disposal. Many executives use and have their own jets and justify it by saying they need

It to be able to get to anywhere in the world at a moment's notice; which they feel is a job requirement for people at the top of organizations. I'm not going to argue for or against that assertion here.

But Jackson took owning his own jet to another level. On one occasion, he decided to fly from the headquarters to a field office at midnight. Since the flight attendant hadn't known about the flight until a few minutes before midnight, she had no time to do any special shopping before the plane left.

Jackson got aboard the jet and after a few minutes said, "Penny, I want a bag of Houser's Potato Chips." She got it for him, but later, being still hungry, he wanted another bag. "I'm sorry, Mr. Jones, but I didn't know about our flight until the last minute so I didn't have time to buy any more Houser's Potato Chips. We do have Wilson's Potato Chips, however. Can I get you a bag of those?"

"No", replied Jackson. "You're fired!" And he actually fired her on the spot. So much for showing genuine concern for employees' welfare.

Still another characteristic of those who show signs of The Phenomenon is feeling one can do no wrong. An example of this is illustrated by a situation that occurred in an organization in the aerospace industry. Results in one division were not good and the CEO, Herbert, was not happy. He called a meeting of the managers and unleashed his vitriol.

"The results this quarter were horrible. It's your fault, not mine. You created this mess, not me. Now you need to clean it up."

The head of HR, who was in the meeting, was tempted to tell the CEO this: That's interesting. But you learn in Management 101 that you can never delegate responsibility, only authority." However, he wanted to keep his job, so he kept his mouth shut.

Herbert made the outrageous statements above because of a simple fact. He felt that he could not possibly be responsible for the "mess" he referred to, because he believed he could do no wrong. If the results were bad, it could not possibly have been because of something he did or didn't do. It must have been the fault of someone else, namely his staff.

What was particularly interesting about this anecdote was that six months later, the results of the division improved significantly. Did Herbert thank or give credit to the managers in the division for the favorable turnaround? No, he did not. Instead, he took full credit for the improvement. He felt that his powerful "motivational speech" did the trick.

Herbert's taking credit for the turnaround in results illustrates another characteristic of those who succumb to The Phenomenon: they believe that everything good that has happened to them or their organizations is because of their brilliance or talents, not due to anyone else or to luck.

Herbert's aerospace company did do very well in terms of growth and profitability over a number of years. However, the success he celebrated was due mainly to the efforts of others and some luck in being in the right place at the right time. As a business psychologist, I can say with some certainty that Herbert's success has been primarily despite his efforts, not because of them. He has violated nearly every principle of effective management. He believes you treat people like dirt, pay them as little as possible, give them minimal benefits, get as much out of them as humanly possible, and then dump them if necessary and get somebody else to replace them. Fortunately, for him, he has gotten some people to work for him who have been very good at their jobs. How he got them to work for him is still a mystery to me.

Another person illustrating the characteristic of believing that everything that has happened to him is the result of his brilliance and talents, not due to anyone else's, was Raymond. Raymond was brought into a multinational, diversified products organization as President to replace the CEO, who was scheduled to retire within a few years. The Board of Directors brought in Raymond because the company was hemorrhaging. Financial losses were great and the future didn't look rosy. Raymond's expertise was finance; having been a successful CFO made the Board believe that he could do the impossible: turn around a sinking ship.

The CEO, Bernard, was as different from Raymond as one could imagine. Bernard was an ebullient, extrovert who loved the limelight. He believed in full communication; the company had quarterly meetings at which employees found out the financial results and could ask any question of the top executive group. There were also other communication vehicles such as the company newsletter. In addition, Bernard had an open door policy and told all employees they could come to his office any time with a question or concern and he would address it.

Bernard's problem, however, was that he liked to spend money. In fact, one of the Presidents of one of Bernard's organization's subsidiary companies once told a group this: "Bernard told me when I started that his job is to spend money. My job is to make money. And he's doing a lot better at his job than I am at mine."

Bernard wanted growth; profitability was a secondary concern. That's why the company was hurting, however.

Raymond, the new President, was a very private introvert. He was the antithesis of Bernard. All he cared about was the bottom line – not about growth or employees. His lack of genuine concern for the welfare of employees was illustrated by this anecdote. Raymond held a meeting for all of the sales managers in the core business. He started the meeting by saying, "I've heard that many of you are not happy about the direction the Sales Department is going in now. Well, my message for you is simple: if you don't like it, then get the hell out!" How's that for showing employees that you are genuinely concerned for their welfare?

The Board gave Raymond license to do whatever was necessary to turn around the situation. He took decisive action. He sold all of the company's international operations. He sold nearly all of the company's facilities. Raymond sold everything outside of the company's historical core business. In one year, the company went from $100 million in the hole to a $50 million profit: a $150 million dollar turnaround. But many people in the company felt he destroyed the backbone of the organization and its people in the process.

He, of course, took complete credit for the company's turnaround. The Board, who supported his actions, and the employees who helped him got no kudos for the dramatic change in the organization's financial position.

Raymond shared a number of additional characteristics with other people who exhibit TP. He didn't listen to anyone else for advice. He had all the answers; why would he need to get anyone else's opinion? He felt he knew everything there was to know about the company's core business.

Raymond also demonstrated another characteristic of people who succumb to The Phenomenon: he had very little empathy for anyone. When he had to cut thousands of employees from the company payroll to achieve what he wanted, did he care about the thousands of families who were hurt? No, he did not. His attitude towards the former employees was, "The hell with them. We didn't need them anyway."

Another person who exhibited a lack of empathy and succumbed to The Phenomenon was Sarah. Sarah was President of a pharmaceutical firm. She was evaluating the health care costs of her firm. When the insurer told her that her premiums would go up by twenty percent, she said that was unacceptable. "How can we change that figure dramatically," she asked. The local representative of the insurance agency that dealt with the company said, "One way we can do that is to change the mental health benefits. People now have thirty days of hospital stay for serious mental health problems, like suicide attempts. We can change that to three days' maximum stay in a hospital, save a ton of money, and drop the premium increase by fifty percent."

The VP of HR felt compelled to tell Sarah and the agency representative that he strongly disagreed with the proposed action. The representative, a true sycophant, who told Sarah only what she wanted to hear, not necessarily the truth, said, "That three day maximum stay won't be a problem. If someone needs more time in the hospital, there are social programs out there that will take care of it."

Despite the head of HR's strong protestations about the proposed benefit program change and his disagreement with the representative's assurances, Sarah decided to go along with the proposed change. "If we can reduce the premium increase by fifty percent, I think it's a great idea," she stated. Her lack of empathy for employees unfortunate enough to have serious mental health problems, such as attempted suicide, was pathetic.

Sarah's insistence on saving money at the expense of the less fortunate illustrated another key characteristic of people who exhibit TP: taking advantage of others for one's own gain. She got a substantial bonus for keeping expenses to a minimal level. It didn't matter that someone else might suffer because of her decision, as long as she made more money.

One more characteristic of people exhibiting The Phenomenon is this: believing that you know not only everything in your own area of expertise where you've had success, you're now an expert on every subject. Politics, religion, whatever: you know all there is to know about everything. These people truly believe that they are God's gift to the world and are overjoyed at the opportunity to share their "wisdom" with everyone, whether their opinion is solicited or not.

Bart was a person who had been a successful banker and he now felt he had the right, no the obligation, to share his views on politics and religion and any other subject with anyone who would listen, and some who would prefer not to hear what he had to say.

I met Bart at a party once. Finding out that I was a psychologist, he informed me that he had read a book on birth order and now, as a result, would not hire anyone in a significant managerial position in his bank unless the person was first-born. I informed him that while research did indicate a modest positive correlation between achievement and being first-born, it was not an appropriate criterion to use for eliminating all sorts of well-qualified candidates for executive roles. Bart simply smiled and dismissed my opinion as erroneous and took his as the gospel. Even though his background was all in banking, not human resources or psychology, he believed he knew more about the subject than someone with a Ph.D. in psychology, an M.B.A. in management, many years of experience as an HR executive and numerous years of experience as a psychologist in business.

Although all of the examples of people exhibiting characteristics of The Phenomenon so far have been executives, as I indicated previously, many others outside of the executive suite also exhibit this malady.

A former colleague of mine told me that he had a good friend who had had a very successful career as a dermatologist. My co-worker said that he and his friend had joked once about the fact that they knew other very successful physicians and attorneys who felt that they now were experts in all areas and loved to pontificate about their great insights. My colleague said that the amazing thing was that his good friend was guilty of the very same behavior they had joked about.

So if there are a lot of people who succumb to TP, how did they get that way? That's the topic of the next chapter.

CHAPTER 2

How Did They Get That Way?

Introduction

The I Know Everything About Everything Phenomenon is a new concept. There is no research on it because it hasn't been identified before. (As I will indicate again later in this book, research needs to be done on The Phenomenon to validate its existence, how it comes into being, how one can measure it, and how it can be changed.)

There have been many debates among psychologists over the years about nature versus nurture. Are we born with various traits or does our environment shape us? The consensus today seems obvious – both heredity and environment have major impacts on who we are.

I believe that the primary cause of The Phenomenon (TP) is environmental in nature. A person will not develop TP unless she becomes very successful in her field. That, at least, is my current theory and this theory, as I indicated above and will state later in this book, needs to be tested.

The reason I theorize that The Phenomenon is a learned concept is that I am familiar with a number of individuals who were very nice, typical, non-narcissistic people earlier their lives – say their 20's and 30's, and before that as well. Take Myron, for example. He was a "good guy" whom I became familiar with when he was in his late 30's. We played golf together a few times and our families spent time with one another.

Myron was a competent marketer who had worked in the pharmaceutical industry. He was ambitious. He once told me he was going to be a multi-millionaire by the time he was 40. He was an executive vice president of a company that made prescription drugs. The company decided to spin off one of its divisions and Myron, along with a few other executives, asked to buy it.

The company had been unionized but Myron and the others felt that they would not be able to run the new organization profitably unless the union was decertified. The decertification went through and the management group, including Myron, the new CEO, was able to make a small profit originally even though the organization, under the previous management, had not been profitable.

Myron and the other executives wanted the company to grow, so they began doing research on a new drug that they thought had great growth potential. When the new drug was finally approved by the FDA, it became very successful and the company grew profitably.

It was at this point that Myron's confidence began to erode into arrogance. He felt that he had been extremely successful so far in business so he started to believe he was an expert in the field. That would have been fine, but he soon began to believe that he knew everything there was to know about business. He was so arrogant at that point that he would have given Mark Zuckerberg advice on how to start and run a technology firm.

Myron's company continued to grow and was profitable. Eventually, he started to believe that he was not only an expert in business, he began to think he knew everything about everything: politics, religion, and every other aspect of life. Myron succumbed to The I Know Everything About Everything Phenomenon.

Success had been a very positive thing originally, but it had eventually eroded into something negative. While his positive accomplishments originally were an asset, they had now become a liability to him. For example, thinking that he knows everything about everything prevents someone from accepting valuable advice from a co-worker. That can end up in making some poor decisions which have deleterious consequences.

An example of this occurred when Myron decided to lay off 150 production people because business was slow. The VP of HR tried to advise him to keep the people on the payroll because business was likely to get better in a few months. But Myron insisted on keeping costs down by laying off the people anyway. A few months later, business improved dramatically and the company needed 150 more people. About 100 of the laid off people, not knowing when or whether they would be called back to work, got other jobs. So it was necessary to find, hire, and train 100 new people. The recruiting, hiring and training costs considerably exceeded the costs of keeping the 150 people on the payroll in the first place. If Myron had listened to his staff member, he could have saved quite a bit of money for the company. But he wouldn't listen to someone else who was an expert in the area of human resources because he thought he knew everything about everything.

Another example of Myron's belief that he knew everything about everything involved the V.P. of Human Resources at Myron's company. The head of HR had a virtually impossible job because he had to manage the function for about 1200 employees by himself, with the only assistance provided by a paraprofessional without a college degree and limited experience in HR.

The appropriate ratio of employees to HR staff was previously thought to be 100 to one but changed to 200 to one in recent years. By this measure, the V.P. was short about four employees. This was particularly true because the company was growing at a rate of 100% per year, so the V.P. had to spend 95% of his time recruiting and selecting key employees. This left little time for all of the other HR functions (e.g., compensation, benefits, employee relations, training and development, etc.).

The V.P. of HR, whom I will call Kevin, told Myron that he was extremely short of staff, so Myron told Kevin to give him a proposal for staff additions. When Kevin said in his proposal that he needed another four people to do the job effectively, Myron stated, "Absolutely not". "You already have added an assistant; that should be plenty." When Kevin indicated that experts in the field of human resources believed that the ratio of 100-200 to one was necessary to do an effective job, Myron indicated that this ratio didn't apply to his company. He believed that he knew much more about HR than the experts in the field, even though he had never worked in that area before, since all of his background was in marketing.

The V.P. of HR later resigned from the company because he had a virtually impossible job. Myron, who believed that he knew everything about everything, was quick to provide career advice.

"You should go into academia instead," he opined. "Business is not for you," he further stated.

When Kevin told Myron that he had worked for three other companies and had been quite successful in all three, Myron told him "Well, you might be able to work in big companies but not in small, fast growing organizations like ours."

Myron believed that he knew everything about everything and that both he and his company were "special", so well-accepted information about the HR function and Kevin's successful record were not relevant.

Another example of a person who exhibited The Phenomenon later in life was Marvin. Marvin was the CEO of a $100 million company. (This was quite a few years ago, so the company would probably have had about $500 million in sales in today's dollars.)

A man, whom I'll call Robin, had worked for Marvin as an executive for quite a few years. He indicated that Marvin had been a good friend and an effective executive earlier in his career. However, he had changed dramatically when he was in 40's, after having experienced significant success, and according to Robin, "became a caricature of his former self". Robin's description of Marvin was very insightful. I had done an executive assessment of Marvin and, although I had not thought of the concept of The Phenomenon at that time, he clearly exhibited signs of it then.

Marvin, since he believed he knew all about everything, did not really utilize all of his executives' talents. Marvin felt that since he was omniscient, he had to make all of the major decisions for his organization. He practiced what a colleague of mine described as "Management by Assistants". In other words, Marvin made all of the key decisions himself and the VP's who worked for him simply implemented them under Marvin's close supervision; they essentially functioned as highly-paid executive assistants.

Another example of a CEO who exhibited symptoms of The Phenomenon and felt he had to make all of the company's significant decisions was Lionel. Lionel ran a multi-billion dollar manufacturing company. He, too, like Marvin, believed he alone was omniscient, so it was necessary for him to make not only major decisions, but also some rather minor ones. For example, Lionel felt that he had to approve the graphic design of the packaging of the company's products.

An additional case study of an individual who exhibited signs of The Phenomenon later in life was "Trey". (He was called this because he was the third person in the family with the same name.) I knew Trey quite well personally and I did consulting for his company, a software manufacturer.

Trey, like Myron, whom I discussed previously, was a "good guy" and a very effective executive when he was in his 20's and 30's. After experiencing a great deal of success in the area of finance, in which he was trained, he became the CEO of a company when he was in his early 40's. The company had been owned by a large conglomerate and then was sold to private investors. Trey was one of a number of executives in the former company who bought a small portion of the new company and also received some additional stock associated with "sweat equity".

Trey and his team had attained very good results in the company when it was owned by the conglomerate. After the company was sold to private investors, including him and his team of executives, the results attained were excellent in terms of substantial sales growth and profitability. After he had accomplished significant things when the company was owned by the conglomerate, Trey began to believe he knew everything about business. After he continued to attain outstanding results, he began to believe he was omniscient and succumbed to TP.

An example of Trey's belief in his omniscience occurred at a party. A woman who was a friend of Trey's had been talking to a home designer about a proposed architectural drawing of her new home. Trey walked up to the two, interrupted the designer, and started giving advice on changing the design. The designer, who also knew Trey, said, "I didn't know you were a home designer, too." In actuality, Trey had had no training or experience in the design of homes but he felt he was omniscient, so he was qualified to give advice about everything.

What The Phenomenon Is not: Narcissistic Personality Disorder (NPD)

Narcissistic Personality Disorder is something diagnosed by psychologists and psychiatrists. It is included in DSM – 5 (The Diagnostic and Statistical Manual of Mental Disorders – Fifth Edition), which was published by the American Psychiatric Association. Many of the characteristics of Narcissistic Personality Disorder are similar to those of people showing signs of The I Know Everything About Everything Phenomenon.

The causes of NPD are unknown but likely to be complex, according to an article on the internet on November 18, 2015 from the Mayo Clinic. One major difference between TP and NPD, however, is when it first manifests itself. According to the Mayo Clinic article, Narcissistic Personality Disorder first appears in the teens or early adulthood. From my observations, on the other hand, The Phenomenon does not initially typically manifest itself until one is in his or her 40's. The examples I gave previously in this chapter included people who I feel did not exhibit highly narcissistic behavior earlier in their careers. Also, my theory is that the primary cause of The Phenomenon is continued success in one's field.

What are the causes of Narcissistic Personality Disorder? As I indicated previously, they are likely to be complex. There are some theories as to the possible causes of N PD, however. L.C. Groopman and A.M. Cooper indicated in 2006 that the following possible causes have been identified by some researchers:

1. Personality traits at birth.
2. A great deal of admiration that is not balanced by feedback that is realistic.

3. Considerable praise for favorable behavior.
4. A great deal of criticism for negative child behavior.
5. Being overindulged or overvalued by key people in their lives (e.g., parents, members of their family, or other children)
6. Getting praise from older people for special abilities or appearance.
7. Being emotionally abused as a child.
8. Having parents that treat them in an unpredictable or unreliable manner.
9. Being taught to be manipulative by parents or other children.
10. Being valued by their parents to aid the self-esteem of the parents.

Groopman and Cooper went on to state that some narcissism is typical in usual development. However, when narcissism is exacerbated by problems in the interpersonal environment, it may be magnified to the point of Narcissistic Personality Disorder.

The following researchers, A. Vater, H.R. Heekeren, M. Bajbouj, B. Renneberg, I. Heuser, and S. Poepke, in a 2013 article in the Journal of Psychiatric Research entitled "Gray Matter Abnormalities in Patients with Narcissistic Personality Disorder", stated that there are structural abnormalities in the brains of people with Narcissistic Personality Disorder. These are particularly noted in areas of the brain which deal with the ability to be empathic and compassionate, the capacity to regulate emotions, and intellectual functioning.

The article on the internet from November 18, 2015 published by the Mayo Clinic referred to previously indicated that some results of Narcissistic Personality Disorder, if left untreated, include the following:

1. Problems with relationships.
2. Difficulties at home or school.
3. Depression.
4. Substance abuse.
5. Suicidal ideation or attempted suicide.

The Mayo Clinic went on to indicate in the article referred to above that a thorough psychological evaluation is necessary to diagnose Narcissistic Personality Disorder. Also, they suggested that a physical examination is also necessary in order to ensure that the symptoms of Narcissistic Personality Disorder are not being caused by physical difficulties.

I have worked with people who have Narcissistic Personality Disorder as well as people demonstrating signs of TP. The first example of someone with Narcissistic Personality Disorder was Sheldon. Sheldon had training in business. He got a bachelor's degree in business and an M.B.A. with an emphasis in human resources.

Sheldon's specialty was employee recruiting. At age 25, he thought he was God's gift to the recruiting field. Sheldon once made a recruiting video. In it, he appeared as the "savior" in a company because he was so amazingly talented at recruiting. He even used the theme from "Rocky" in the last part of the video. He had no clue that people who viewed the video were so appalled by his hubris that they almost regurgitated with disgust.

Sheldon was narcissistic about his body as well. He pumped iron regularly so that he could show off his bulging biceps and pecs. Naturally, he felt he was quite a "catch" when it came to the ladies. At one point, Sheldon had three young women all fighting with one another over who had dibs on him.

Sheldon's narcissism led him to try to market his recruiting services to outside organizations, despite the fact that the company that employed him had its own recruiting services subsidiary. He saw no obvious conflict of interest in this case.

Sheldon told his boss's secretary, who handled his expenses, that it was difficult for him to "get motivated" to turn in his expense report. She told her boss, "Boy, Sheldon really is a total jerk."

Sheldon once did a joint presentation out of town on recruiting with a coworker. The coworker came in at 7 a.m. because the presentation was scheduled to begin at 8 a.m. He wanted to make sure that the room was set up properly, the AV equipment was available, etc. Sheldon, however, did not deign to make his presence known until 7:55 a.m. When questioned about why he did not show up at 7 a.m. he said, "Well, I thought you would do that stuff." Sheldon felt that he was "special" so that he didn't need to bother himself with cumbersome details regarding the presentation.

Finally, Sheldon had angered so many people with his narcissism that his supervisor was going to terminate his employment. Sheldon, however, apparently could sense that things were not going well for him, so he resigned the night before he was going to be fired.

Since Sheldon thought he was more brilliant than everyone else, he expected that he would be a resounding success as an entrepreneur. Sheldon started his own recruiting company in a grandiose, rather than a prudent, manner. He hired numerous recruiters so he would have a major firm right off the bat. However, he didn't bother to get a base of clients first. When a former co-worker saw Sheldon at an airport, he admitted that he had a huge staff with only limited revenue. It was astounding that Sheldon actually admitted that he was not spectacular at something.

Sheldon gave clear indications that he had Narcissistic Personality Disorder when he was in his mid-20's. He probably demonstrated signs of NPD even earlier, but I didn't meet him until he was 25. Some of his symptoms included the following:

1. He was extremely arrogant.
2. He was incapable of seeing things from anyone else's perspective.
3. He thought he was "special" so the rules didn't apply to him.
4. He believed he had exceptional talents that were far superior to those of others.
5. He believed he was "above" mundane activities that others had to do.
6. He "used" others for his personal gain.

Sheldon was primarily different from those who have symptoms of The Phenomenon because he exhibited his narcissistic symptoms early in life, long before he had a substantial track record of significant accomplishments. Sheldon didn't exhibit egocentric symptoms because he had had years of successful experience in his field. He demonstrated them because of his innate belief that he was superior to others.

Another example of a person with Narcissistic Personality Disorder was Beau. I worked with Beau also when it was fairly early in his career (he was in his early 30's). Beau had a bachelor's degree in business and an M.B.A. in human resources management. His specialty area was employee relations.

When I first met Beau he had been an employee relations specialist for a firm in the Midwest. He then took a job as an employee relations manager for another company in the heartland.

Beau loved calling attention to himself. I had to chuckle when my three-year-old first met him. Beau had a gold chain around his neck and my son grabbed the chain and said, "Ooh, K-Mart!"

Speaking of gold, Beau more than once made a comment about a gold-plated pen I had gotten when I worked at the Parker Pen Company. He repeatedly told me, "You're so lucky!" My thought at the time he said this was simply, "So I have a gold-plated pen. Big deal."

Beau "used" people regularly to get what he wanted. On one occasion, he asked another member of the HR Department to help him put in a lawn at his new home. The coworker was working hard raking the soil when Beau announced that he had to leave for an appointment. He didn't see any problem with having the coworker continue to strive on his lawn, despite the fact that Beau was "too busy" to continue to work on it.

Beau volunteered to work on a special project for his company involving a major reorganization. Everyone else who was working on the project got meager accommodations so that they could be in close proximity with one another. Beau, of course, being so important, had to have palatial accommodations. He talked the head of the project into letting him create an office right next to the CEO's. Beau claimed that it was necessary for him to be there so he would have easy access to the CEO during the project.

Beau's inability to empathize and see things from others' perspective was made clear regarding his lack of punctuality concerning meetings. He was late to virtually every meeting scheduled. Typically, he was not just a few minutes late, but often 20-30 minutes tardy. On one occasion, his staff waited nearly an hour for him to show up.

One of Beau's supervisors highlighted his tardiness on one occasion. He locked the door to the room where the meeting was held. So when Beau arrived twenty minutes late as usual, he had to bang on the door for two minutes before his boss let him in. You would think that after the aforementioned embarrassing moment, Beau would have learned his lesson regarding his lack of punctuality. But sadly, he continued to be late for nearly all meetings.

In addition to being late constantly, Beau nearly always waited until the last minute to implement actions. When he needed help from others to do something, which was nearly all the time, he typically gave them the information they needed about one day before the actions needed to be completed.

Beau needed frequent assistance from a graphic designer in the company before he had to make presentations. Being extremely narcissistic, he always expected her to place his projects at the top of the priority list, regardless of what else she had to do. He often invoked the CEO's name when he wanted the graphic designer to do his work immediately.

On one occasion, Beau wanted her to do something on a Sunday evening and asked her supervisor to call her regarding this. The supervisor refused to do this and told Beau that while he was willing to be called on a Sunday evening, she was not a highly-paid person and should not be bothered at this time to do Beau's bidding.

Beau had an assistant working for him on the reorganization project. Beau, as usual, was unable to empathize with his assistant, so he routinely called for meetings with the two of them on Sunday evening at 9 p.m. It did not occur to Beau, because of his extreme egocentrism, that his assistant might want to spend time with his family on Sunday evenings at 9 p.m.

Beau's supervisor was fired when he got a new boss. When the new supervisor moved to the area and was scheduled to start, he was very ill. Beau, naturally, wanted to get an audience immediately to "sell" himself to his new supervisor. When the man told Beau that he was very ill and begged off, Beau insisted that they had to meet immediately, despite the man's illness. His new boss had heard numerous stories about Beau's shortcomings, so he had planned to fire Beau as one of his first undertakings in the new job. Beau's insistence on meeting immediately, despite his new supervisor's illness, only reinforced his decision to get rid of Beau. Beau was quite surprised when the first thing out of his boss's mouth when they met was, "You're fired!"

After Beau left the company, he tried to sell himself as an expert on a novel system of supervision. A woman who had worked for Beau was an expert regarding the system. Beau's understanding of the system, however, was minimal at best. So he had to try to "use" her by trying to convince her to come with him to a new employer. By promising her everything under the sun, he was successful in his efforts.

After he was there for a few months, his new employer recognized that Beau really had little understanding of the novel system of supervision. They realized that they needed only the woman he had convinced to join him, not Beau. Beau was let go and needed to try to do a "sales job" on his talents to other potential employers.

Beau experienced only limited success in his career, so he did not develop The Phenomenon. He clearly had Narcissistic Personality Disorder, however. His symptoms included the following:

1. Loving to call attention to himself.
2. Being jealous of others who had things he desired.
3. "Using" others to his advantage.
4. Lacking empathy regarding how others perceived his behavior.
5. Believing that he deserved "special" treatment.
6. Being concerned with only what he wanted, not what others might desire.
7. Taking credit for others' talents.

Why do some people exhibit The Phenomenon while others do not?

It is uncertain why some people develop TP while others do not. This is an issue that needs to be researched further. My theory is that it depends on how a person explains her success. If someone believes that her success is due to her brilliance and talents alone, she may develop the Phenomenon. If, on the other hand, someone believes that her success is due to not only her attributes but also to the efforts and success of others, as well as some possible good fortune (i.e., luck), she probably will not succumb to The Phenomenon.

An example of one individual who did not develop The Phenomenon was James. I first met James when he was in his early 40's. He had been very successful in his career up to that point. He had been with only one employer since he graduated from college. He started as a manufacturing specialist with his organization. He was promoted to a production supervisor earlier in his career. He then advanced to the Manager of Manufacturing, and then later became Vice President of Manufacturing.

I was involved with James as a coach early in my career. I did an assessment of James using an in-depth interview and various psychological tests. I found that despite James' significant success in his career, he maintained considerable humility. He did not believe that he advanced rapidly solely due to his talents. Rather, he thought that he did well career-wise not just due to his aptitude but also because he had very talented people working for him and above him who helped him succeed.

James went on to head up worldwide operations for his organization. Even then, however, he retained his humble attitude and never felt he knew everything about operations and certainly never believed he was omniscient.

A second example of a very successful person who never developed symptoms of The Phenomenon was John. John was Senior Vice President of Marketing for his company. When I first met John, he was about 50 years old. He started out as a marketing specialist. He then advanced to product manager, then V.P. of Marketing, and finally, Senior V.P. of Worldwide Marketing.

Like James, John did not believe that his career advancement was due solely to his numerous talents. Instead, John remained humble despite his success career-wise. He, like James, believed that he was able to advance significantly in his career because of extremely talented supervisors and staff members and some luck.

A third example of someone who was very successful in her career but did not develop symptoms of The Phenomenon was Susan. Susan began her career after graduating from college in the Federal Government as an employee of the Agency for International Development (AID). After spending a year or two with AID, she joined a company as a product specialist. The organization recognized her talent, so they promoted her to product manager. She then was promoted again to Vice President of a group of products.

The organization she worked for was well known for its industrial products, so an executive recruiter identified her as an excellent candidate for a job as the President of a start-up company in the large manufacturing equipment industry.

Susan experienced extreme success in her start up. She told me that she started with a staff of ten people and built it into an organization of 25,000 people. Susan stepped down when the company had grown to 25,000 employees. She then started another company, which is still growing significantly today.

Susan, like James and John, maintained her humility despite significant career success. She knew that she could not have accomplished what she did without having extremely supportive supervisors and very talented, hard-working staff members.

Getting back to The I Know Everything About Everything Phenomenon, in what ways do characteristics of The Phenomenon affect individuals exhibiting it? This topic is covered in the next chapter.

CHAPTER 3

HOW DO PEOPLE WHO EXHIBIT THE PHENOMENON AFFECT THEMSELVES AND OTHERS?

How it affects them

My hypothesis is that people exhibiting The Phenomenon have relatively normal childhoods. Of course, they would exhibit some narcissistic behavior as children, because all kids start out their lives being rather self-centered. It is only after the socialization process kicks in that children begin to realize that the whole world does not revolve around them and that they need to take others' needs into account as well.

I also hypothesize that people exhibiting The Phenomenon have a relatively normal adolescence. Once again, they may exhibit some egocentric behavior from time to time, but by and large, they are tuned into what other people want and need as well as what they themselves desire.

I believe that people who exhibit TP also have a relatively normal early adulthood. In Chapter II, I discussed examples of people I knew who were good, non-narcissistic individuals when they were in their 20's and 30's, but who later showed signs of The Phenomenon after they had experienced significant success in their careers. After they started to succumb to The Phenomenon, all three exhibited various symptoms of TP, including the following:

- They were extremely arrogant.
- They thought they knew everything about their area of expertise.
- They would not admit it when they made mistakes.
- They didn't listen to advice from people who knew a lot more about an area of expertise that they did.
- They felt they were "special" and that the rules and laws didn't apply to them.
- They didn't demonstrate concern for employees.
- They felt that they were "better" than everyone else.
- They felt they could do no wrong.
- They believed that everything favorable that occurred was solely the result of their brilliance and talents.
- They had little empathy for others.
- They took advantage of others for their personal gain.
- They believed they knew everything about everything.

What happens to those exhibiting The Phenomenon if they become unsuccessful?

The above is an interesting question. I would hypothesize that at least a few of those people might modify their deleterious behavior to some extent. If, as I believe, continued success is what causes The Phenomenon, then no longer being successful might tend to precipitate eliminating at least some TP behavior.

Undoubtedly, however, some people exhibiting The Phenomenon might continue showing their extremely obnoxious behavior. They might convince themselves that the lack of success was not due to what they did or failed to do. As a result, they would continue to believe that they know everything about everything and are "special" individuals.

How it affects others

The Phenomenon has an extremely adverse impact on co-workers. Imagine being the head of marketing for an organization. Let's say you have been in the field for thirty years and have been extremely successful in several previous marketing positions in other organizations. Your current boss, the CEO, shows many signs of The Phenomenon. So when a marketing decision has to be made and you make a recommendation, he vetoes it every time, even though he has never worked in marketing before, since his entire background had been in manufacturing before becoming a CEO.

He vetoes your prudent decisions, because he believes he knows everything there is to know about marketing, as well as every other business function. How would you feel? Possibly demoralized, angry, and staring to question your expertise and confidence in your area? That is how many people feel who have a person exhibiting behavior associated with The Phenomenon as supervisors.

Let's discuss another example outside of business. Suppose you are a medical doctor who has been practicing as a successful, board-certified cardiac surgeon for twenty years. You are about to perform heart surgery on a patient using a new technique that has been documented as being superior to the "old", traditional way of doing the surgery. You have been fully trained in the new technique but the Chief of Surgery has not gone through the training. She exhibits symptoms of The Phenomenon and believes she knows everything about surgery, questions the use of the new technique and orders you to do the surgery the traditional way. How would you feel? Probably the way the Marketing V.P. in the previous example felt: angry, demoralized, and possibly questioning your expertise.

What about how someone feels who is a family member of an individual exhibiting symptoms of TP? Suppose you are the spouse of such a person. You are a professional chef at a well-known, successful gourmet restaurant and have been there for fifteen years.

You are cooking dinner for your spouse, an attorney who has no culinary training. However, he exhibits TP: he believes he knows everything about everything, including gourmet cooking. He says, "You are using too much olive oil in that recipe." How would you feel? Probably similar to the way the people in the previous examples felt.

Let's discuss another example of a family member of someone clearly demonstrating TP behavior. Suppose you are the daughter of a tenured college professor at a prestigious university. You are twenty-one years old and have been a successful professional model for five years. Your mother, the professor, knows nothing about modeling and very little about clothing but believes she is omniscient. Your mother is visiting you and you are going out on a date. Your mother says, "That outfit is all wrong on you!" How would you feel? Let's put it this way: You probably wouldn't be feeling a strong urge to nominate her for Mother of the Year.

Friends of people exhibiting signs of The Phenomenon also are adversely affected. Suppose you are a well-known, accomplished architect with twenty-five years of experience. A close friend, a dentist who exhibits numerous signs of The Phenomenon is talking to you about designing his new office building. You come up with a design that you spent many hours on. He critiques it, finding six alleged design flaws, even though he has no training or expertise in architecture. How would you feel? You probably would not have a burning desire to go out and have a drink with your buddy.

We have seen how exhibiting symptoms of The I Know Everything About Everything Phenomenon can adversely affect the person, his co-workers, his family, and his friends. What are some of the places where we can find those who succumb to The Phenomenon? I will address that in more detail in the next chapter.

CHAPTER 4

WHERE CAN WE FIND THOSE WHO SUCCUMB TO THE PHENOMENON?

Business executives

Obviously there are some CEO's who exhibit characteristics of The Phenomenon. In the first three chapters, numerous examples of CEO's who succumbed to this malady were provided.

Clearly, there are some other non-CEO executives who exhibit symptoms of The Phenomenon as well. One example of this is the unnamed financial executive discussed in Chapter I, who refused to admit his mistakes. As you may recall, he tried to solve the problem of experienced production workers complaining about the fact that the new people were paid the same wage. His totally inappropriate solution was to reduce the wage of the new production people, rather than increasing the wage of experienced individuals. It had already been hard to recruit decent new people at the previous wage. When it became even more difficult to recruit decent new production employees after implementing his idea, he refused to admit that his solution was a poor one.

Another example of an executive who exhibited symptoms of the Phenomenon was Fred. Fred was a quality control executive in manufacturing. Whenever someone would ask why something either inside or outside of the quality control area occurred, Fred <u>always</u> gave an explanation for it. He felt he was omniscient and knew everything there was to know about not only quality control but also every other aspect of business.

Academicians

Some professors also succumb to The I Know Everything About Everything Phenomenon. Two of these individuals in the area of sociology once gave a talk on charisma. They started out by making the assumption that both of them, obviously, had this characteristic. They exhibited the extreme arrogance that those who exhibit characteristics of The Phenomenon have.

Another professor exhibited an additional characteristic that some people who show signs of The Phenomenon demonstrate: he manipulated others and took advantage of them for his personal gain.

On one occasion this history professor, whom we will call Paul, invited a group of graduate students to his cottage in Central Wisconsin. He expected everyone to stay there the entire weekend, from Friday evening through Sunday afternoon. When one doctoral student, Art, told Paul that he was leaving late Saturday afternoon to go back to Milwaukee for a university basketball game, Paul asked him to reconsider his decision. Art asked Paul, "Do I <u>have</u> to skip the game and stay here tonight?" Paul arrogantly replied, "Art, I can't <u>make</u> you do anything. I can just make you <u>wish</u> that you had."

Paul also coerced all of the graduate students who had him as an advisor to go drinking with him regularly because he wanted company. Paul always paid for all of everyone's drinks. This happened not because he was especially generous but because he wanted to overcome the objection most of his students would have expressed: "But I can't go drinking because I have no money." One unfortunate student, who was married when he was in graduate school, almost ended up being divorced by his wife because Paul made him go drinking with him so often, he could not spend substantial time with her.

Those in government

As I mentioned in Chapter I, this book is apolitical in that I do not wish to use it to endorse or bash any politician. However, without naming names, it appears that there are some people who are in upper levels of government who exhibit signs of The Phenomenon.

One well-known individual who is an upper-level government official exhibits extreme arrogance and seems to feel that he knows everything about everything.

Another well-known individual, who had been in upper-level government appeared to have felt that she was "special" and that the rules that applied to others did not apply to her, based on her past behavior.

You do not need to look far in current Federal, state, or local government to find numerous other individuals who exhibit various symptoms of The Phenomenon. For example, one member of upper-level state government, whom we will call George, made a special effort to eliminate unions for teachers. In doing so, George exhibited a lack of empathy for teachers, and the impact on their families, of such an effort.

Another former member of upper-level state government seemed to exhibit a characteristic of The Phenomenon – namely, that he knew everything about everything. This person, whom we will call Tom, was very successful as a college professor. He was an excellent lecturer, so students flocked to his classes. Tom appeared to believe that he knew everything about teaching because of his success.

After experiencing more success in academia, Tom began to feel he knew everything about everything. As a result, he felt that he could run a university without any problem. So he applied for, and got, an appointment as the head of a university.

After experiencing success in the role, Tom believed that he could be successful in business, so he applied for, and got, a position as the President of a major corporation.

Unfortunately, Tom was not as successful as a top-level business executive as he had been in his former roles. He was asked to resign from his role as President by the CEO. In retrospect, I feel that Tom being asked to step down was not necessarily due to his lack of success as a business executive. Tom's wife was an extremely independent person. When asked by the CEO to participate in various functions, she refused. I believe that his being asked to resign was due more to his wife's intransigence than his lack of performance in his role.

In any case, his situation sheds light on a question brought up in Chapter III – namely, what happens to someone exhibiting symptoms of The Phenomenon when he becomes unsuccessful. I mentioned in that chapter that I believed that some people might tend to exhibit fewer symptoms of TP after their lack of success.

In Tom's case, he may have become more modest in that he chose to not apply for another job as a business executive. Instead, he decided to parlay his past success as a lecturer/professor into a career as a professional public speaker.

Tom was outstanding in this area. I believe he was probably the best public speaker I have ever witnessed. I saw Tom after he became a professional speaker and he told me this. "This is the greatest legal scam around. I'm still giving lectures like I did at the university, but now I'm getting $ 5000 for each one."

Physicians

In Chapter I, I mentioned that a former colleague of mine was a good friend of a physician and that they talked about how some of the doctor's friends, after experiencing continued success as physicians, began to believe that they were not only experts in medicine, but that they also knew everything about every other subject as well. I went on to say that my colleague marveled at the fact that his doctor friend could see this in others, but he did not recognize that he, too, exhibited this characteristic.

Another physician I had contact with, Leonard, was an otolaryngologist (ear, nose, and throat specialist). I had some trouble breathing so he suggested that I have surgery to deal with the deviated septum I got because of a brief, unfortunate stint as a boxer in intracollegiate competition.

After the surgery, Leonard packed my nose with gauze. I went to his office a few days later to have him remove the gauze. Although he did put a rubber apron on me, he did not say anything the amount of bleeding I might experience after the gauze was removed. When he took it out, blood began pouring out of both nostrils. I have an automatic reaction when I see tons of blood pouring out of me – I start to faint. Leonard caught me before I fell to the floor. However, he then demonstrated the extreme lack of empathy some people having signs of The Phenomenon exhibit. He said, "Well, it's a good thing you didn't go to Viet Nam." I was appalled at his comment.

My primary care physician, when he heard about what Leonard had said to me, read him the riot act and told him he had to apologize to me, which he did. Apparently, being an EN&T specialist in a smaller community was not Leonard's dream job because the last I heard, he left to become a plastic surgeon doing breast implant surgery on the West Coast.

Attorneys

Lawyers are not immune to The I Know Everything About Everything Phenomenon. I saw one tax attorney whom I worked with at the office one day, so I asked him if he wanted to attend one of my management development sessions. I gave him the date, but rather than just say, "I can make it or I'm busy that day", he said, "Send me a memo on that." I felt that this demonstrated a lack of empathy, one characteristic of those exhibiting signs of the Phenomenon, since it required me to go through extra effort. However, I did what he asked. Later that day I received a memo from him that simply said, "I can't attend because I'm busy that day." I wondered why he could not have just told me that when I asked him face-to-face.

The same individual, whom we'll call Stan, exhibited another characteristic of those showing signs of the CEO Phenomenon:

extreme arrogance. He regularly sent memos to the CEO telling him how much money his tax ideas saved the corporation. Although he either didn't know this or didn't care, this action really turned off the CEO, so it did not aid Stan's career.

Dentists

Some people in the dental profession also exhibit signs of The Phenomenon. One dentist I am familiar with developed an extremely successful practice. Initially, his success made him feel he knew everything about the field of dentistry. Later, as he enjoyed continued financial and professional success, he began to believe that he was an expert in all aspects of life. Although he had no training or expertise in the field of education, he apparently considered himself to be an expert in that domain. One day, he made the following pronouncements about teachers: "They are way overpaid. First of all, they get three months off every year. No other job gives you all summer off. Secondly, how hard is it to teach?" My wife, Lynn, a speech and language pathologist who worked in the schools, also taught in the classroom and was outstanding in her field; she would vigorously dispute his assertions.

Engineers

I have worked with quite a few engineers in my career (and I also authored a book entitled Managing Engineers and Technical Employees). They, too, are not exempt from The Phenomenon.

One man I coached, Kevin, was a mechanical engineer and manager. He had no education, training, or experience in the area of human resources, but he believed he knew everything about all functional areas of business, so HR was no exception.

Kevin thought he was an expert in employee selection. One person who interviewed for a job in Kevin's area, was an older individual. Kevin vetoed the man for the job. When the head of HR asked why he didn't want to employ the man, Kevin said, "Because he smells like my cousin, who had cancer. I know he must have cancer too, so we need to forget about hiring him." The head of HR was so astounded at Kevin's pronouncement, he was speechless.

Kevin apparently believed that his nose was as sensitive as some dogs, who can actually detect some types of cancer in patients with substantial accuracy. In fact, dogs' sense of smell is 10,000 to 100,000 times as acute as humans', according to scientists. Kevin, apparently, was part beagle and he also succumbed to The I Know Everything About Everything Phenomenon.

Psychologists

Unfortunately, even some people in my field exhibit characteristics of The Phenomenon. I encountered one such individual, Michael, earlier in my career.

Michael was a psychologist and professor. He consulted at a prison in Wisconsin, so one day he invited several graduate students, including me, to accompany him to the penitentiary. It was a very interesting day; I got to sit in on a parole hearing and some of my classmates got to witness a group therapy session with inmates.

When all of us were meeting with the prison psychologist, I asked him whether anyone had ever escaped from there. Before he could reply, Michael said, "I read about one person who successfully escaped from here about two years ago and was never found, according to the Milwaukee Journal." The psychologist said, "I don't think that's true, but let's call the Warden, who has been here for the past twenty years."

After talking to this boss, the prison psychologist said, "Yes, the Warden confirmed that no one has ever successfully escaped. He did say that one man tried to hide in a garbage can about ten years ago. However, to discourage prisoners from trying that, correctional officers always shoved sharp, spear-like sabers down into the garbage cans before they were taken away. When the can was emptied at the dump some time later, the inmate was discovered. He had almost bled to death and was returned to the prison."

Michael exhibited one sign of The Phenomenon: he refused to admit that he could make an error. Instead of admitting that he was wrong, he replied, "Well I guess the Milwaukee Journal must have made a mistake."

Michael demonstrated numerous characteristics of the CEO Phenomenon. His arrogance was lengendary. Michael was an adjunct professor at a medical school. I once talked to one of his students, who referred to Michael as a "pompous ass".

Michael loved to demonstrate how intelligent he was by showing off his extremely extensive vocabulary. (Michael might say that he was grandiloquent.) On an occasion in one of my classes, he used an adjective to describe something and then went on to use eight other fancy-sounding synonyms for that adjective to make his point in his typical, pompous manner.

Michael believed that he knew everything there was to know about vocabulary. One of my fellow students once used a word that apparently wasn't in the dictionary and Michael said, "Bill, that word is between you and God."

Sports figures

Professional athletes are the best in the world at their sport. Those who excel in professional sports are the best-of-the-best. The latter athletes probably have the right to be cocky about their expertise in their respective sport. However, when they go beyond their sport and start to believe they are almost God-like in terms of their knowledge of everything under the sun, then they enter the realm of The Phenomenon.

One well-known, former professional basketball player, a member of the Hall of Fame, whom we'll call Stanley, regularly made outrageous statements. They related to his apparent belief that he knew everything about everything. He exhibited the cardinal trait of The Phenomenon.

On one occasion, he was attempting to defend a black professional athlete who was charged with physically abusing his young son. Stanley, in his inimical manner of saying outrageous things, made an inane comment indicating that all black parents in the South beat their children.

Historical figures

Various people in history appear to also have succumbed to The Phenomenon, based on their comments and what others have said about them. First, Adolf Hitler, probably one of the most hated individuals in all of history, seemed to fit in this category. Hitler's megalomania, a characteristic of some with the Phenomenon, was apparent in the following quote attributed to him: "Who says I am not under the special protection of God?" Another quote attributed to Hitler was in a similar vein: "I believe today that my conduct is in accordance with the will of the Almighty Creator."

Hitler's extreme arrogance and his belief that he could do anything were illustrated by the following quote: "If you tell a big enough lie and tell it frequently enough, it will be believed." (All three of the aforementioned Hitler quotes were from Quote Sigma, January 7, 2015).

Hitler's total lack of empathy for others, another characteristic of some who demonstrate signs of The Phenomenon, was obvious from his ordering of the genocide of millions of Jews.

Other figures from history also showed characteristics of The I Know Everything About Everything Phenomenon. Take King Henry VIII of England, for example. He felt he was "special" and the rules did not apply to him, one of the aspects of The Phenomenon. He could not marry Ann Boleyn because he had been married to Queen Catherine. When Pope Clement VII told Henry VIII that he would not annul his marriage to Queen Catherine, Henry decided that he would break the Church of England from Rome's rule, according to Britannica.com

Another historical figure who demonstrated signs of The Phenomenon was the famous general, George S. Patton, Jr. Patton was extremely arrogant, as are most who succumb to TP. According to Martin Blumenson's and Kevin Hymel's biography of Patton, he believed that his family was great and that others were inferior (from Patton: Legendary Commander, p. 17).

Benito Mussolini was another figure from history who showed definite signs of The Phenomenon. He was so cocky that he loved his title of "Little Caesar". He believed he was the reincarnation of a Roman Emperor, according to Don Jaide on December 22, 2009 (from Rosta Livermore on the Internet). Thus, he apparently believed he was "special", another characteristic of those who exhibit TP.

If individuals showing signs of The Phenomenon have been somewhat ubiquitous throughout history, one might wonder, "How can you change individuals demonstrating this behavior?" That is the subject of the next chapter.

CHAPTER 5

HOW CAN THE EFFECTS OF THE PHENOMENON BE MINIMIZED?

Introduction

The title of this chapter reminds me of a question from one of the people whom I coached. I explained my coaching program and he said, "But I have been like this for forty-five years. How can I change my personality?" I replied, "I'm not trying to change your personality. That would be extremely difficult to do and would probably take a few years. However, I believe that people can change certain <u>behavior</u> if they really want to do so. And that can be done in a relatively short period of time. That's what we're trying to do here."

I believe that anyone can change as least some aspects of his behavior if he really wants to. People who exhibit The Phenomenon in its most extreme forms represent the greatest challenge in terms of behavior change. They believe they know everything about everything and that they can do no wrong. So obviously it follows that they wouldn't need to change their behavior because they believe there is nothing wrong with what they do. Secondly, they typically don't have any incentive to change their behavior because they are not aware of how what they do adversely affects themselves and others. However, I believe it is possible for even extreme cases to modify their behavior.

In order for someone who exhibits signs of The Phenomenon to change, there are two requirements:

1) Someone whom he trusts and cares about has to convince him that some of his behavior is having an adverse effect on himself, the trusted person, and others.

2) The person needing to change has to find a qualified, experienced external change agent. Ideally this change agent is an experienced business psychologist who specializes in coaching executives and other successful people. Although this is something I do, I'm not trying to drum up business; there are many people who meet the criteria I just specified.

It is possible for this change agent to be a non-business psychologist, but she would have to be someone who has a significant understanding of successful people in business and other endeavors. She also would need to be very experienced and have a noteworthy track record of coaching others.

How the coaching process works

My approach or model regarding coaching is not the only one that works, but I want to present it here as an example of how people exhibiting The I Know Everything About Everything Phenomenon can change.

I first meet with the individual to describe the process. How they get to me is typically the result of someone else determining that certain aspects of their behavior need to change. That person could be a member of the Board of Directors in the case of a CEO. In the case of a physician, it could be the President of the organization that employs him. In the case of a member of upper management, it could be the CEO of the organization. I have worked with CEO's who initiated the process themselves. Often this occurs because the individual wants to change certain aspects of his behavior but also wants to serve as an example to others in his organization whom he wants to go through the coaching process.

The first step in the process is an in-depth assessment of the person. I do this by using several instruments. The first is an in-depth, biographical interview that covers the person's entire working career, including his educational background that prepared him for the field. The interview typically takes 2 to 2.5 hours to complete.

Next, the person being assessed takes four instruments:

1) A test of critical thinking;
2) A test of leadership style and effectiveness;
3) A personality inventory; and
4) An inventory of behavioral styles.

In addition, the assessee takes a 360 degree feedback tool I developed called the Management Assessment and Development Inventory (the MADI). I have used the MADI for over 30 years. It is an 87 item inventory that measures various aspects of management including planning, decision-making, communicating, leading, and developing others. I also have a shorter inventory called the Employee Assessment and Development Inventory (the EADI) which is used with non-managers. It has a similar format and includes some of the same questions as the MADI and some other ones relevant to those who do not have managerial responsibilities.

The individuals rate themselves and then they distribute about ten forms to others with whom they work closely, including staff members, peers, and supervisors.

The individual's self-ratings on each item can be compared to the mean of co-worker ratings. The assessee can also see the distribution of co-worker ratings on the five point scale ranging from little to no extent (1) to a very great extent (5). The assessee can also see the deviation between the self-ratings and those of co-workers.

After the various tests and inventories are scored, I analyze these results and the in-depth interview and develop a report on the person. It includes four sections:

1) Personal characteristics and capabilities;
2) Managerial and professional competence;
3) Potential; and
4) Developmental needs.

This report is given to the individual's supervisor. (A similar report is given to the individual, which includes two sections: 1) key strengths; and 2) developmental needs.) The report given to the supervisor contains key test and inventory results. This report is also discussed with the supervisor.

I then meet with the person assessed and review the results of each test and inventory in detail. I also go over the report of key strengths and developmental needs, which includes information from both the interview and the tests/inventories.

Next, I ask the assessee to design an action plan that addresses all of the developmental needs. I ask the person to make the plan specific and measurable, with deadline dates. For example, one of someone's developmental needs might be: "To become more effective at dealing with work-related stress." One possible way to address this is the following action: "After checking with my doctor and getting her approval, exercise at least 30 minutes per day, three times a week, beginning next Monday, September 30th." The above example seems to be quite simple, but it can be extremely effective in aiding someone in managing stress more effectively.

I ask the person assessed to give me a deadline date for designing the developmental action plan. It is essential that the person come up with the plan himself because that leads to ownership on his part. I could easily design a plan myself, but then it would be Doug Soat's plan, not Herb Johnson's plan.

I do review each person's action plan, however, and give him or her suggestions for improvement. After the assessee has included my suggestions in a revised action plan, I ask him or her to implement it.

After this, we meet once a month for about one to two hours to review their progress, or lack thereof, on the developmental action plan. If she is doing well regarding one of the action steps, I give her positive feedback. If she is having problems with an action step, I may suggest alternatives.

After we meet for the sixth time, I ask the person to complete the MADI (or EADI) process once again. We meet and review the results and then I ask him to design a revised action plan. Once again, I review the revised plan and may have some suggestions for improvement. Then he comes up with a revision of the revised plan, and I then ask him to implement it. That ends the coaching process.

Examples of successful coaching
I would like to share some examples of coaching individuals where the process has worked well.

The first example involves a man I will call Frank. Frank was V.P. of Manufacturing at a manufacturer of aircraft parts. His case was brought to my attention by the CEO, who said that although many things Frank did were effective, some of his behavior was causing significant problems for the CEO and other executives. As a result, the CEO said Frank needed to participate in my coaching program. He added that if Frank's behavior in a number of key areas did not improve, his employment would be terminated.

Frank, after being told that he was on very shaky ground and needed to improve considerably to continue his employment, was quite motivated to modify his behavior.

Frank was having problems in a number of areas. For example, he was not meeting his commitments. Someone would ask him to send something to him ASAP and he would say, "Okay. I'll send it to you by next Friday." But next Friday would come and Frank would not have sent the person what he had requested.

Frank designed a developmental action plant that was the most detailed, lengthy one that I had ever seen. It was about five pages long and covered each concern that the CEO and other executives had complained about.

After about a month, Frank's behavior in all of the key developmental needs areas had changed dramatically for the better. He was not only able to keep his job, he became the most effective Vice President on the CEO's staff.

Another person who changed his behavior dramatically via my coaching process was Bob. His supervisor, the head of the organization, was extremely frustrated with him. Bob, too, was on extremely shaky ground. The CEO told me, "Although he is very effective in his job as General Manager of one of the regional offices, he can be extremely abrasive to me. I am not going to put up with it much longer. Can you help?"

The CEO went on to say that, for example, he would come up with a new process that needed to be implemented in the entire organization. As soon as Bob received word about it, he would immediately call up the CEO and say, "This new process is stupid. It doesn't make sense, and I don't want to implement it."

Bob's initial meeting with me went as badly as any I had ever had. In his typical abrasive manner, Bob stated, "The only reason I'm participating in this coaching program is that the CEO is making me do it. I think it's a bunch of B.S."

I assured Bob that the coaching program was a means to help him improve his performance rather than a punitive measure. By the time Bob had gotten feedback from the tests, inventories, and in-depth interview, he began to believe that I was there to help him. He designed a very detailed, specific action plan that addressed his developmental needs, particularly his abrasiveness towards the CEO. One of the ideas he came up with helped him considerably in terms of his immediate impulsive responses to the CEO's proposed actions. He proposed that instead of picking up the phone and instantly berating the CEO's new idea, he would instead spend twenty to thirty minutes engaging in a mundane activity that was not really his job but saved his people time. The company was a plumbing contractor, so Bob would pull together the materials the plumber would need to do a particular job.

By the time he finished the activity, he had calmed down considerably. As a result, he could still respond to the CEO's new idea, but it was by means of a thoughtful, non-abrasive missive.

Bob, who had initially been totally opposed to the coaching process, spent several hours with me in each of the coaching sessions held after he implemented his developmental action plan. He responded to the process more favorably than anyone else whom I had coached up to that time. The CEO was very pleased because Bob's behavior had improved dramatically.

A third example of a successful coaching outcome involved a person named Jill. Jill was a project manager for an electrical contractor. She was fairly effective in her job, but her performance was hampered by a lack of self-confidence and assertiveness.

In designing an action plan, Jill addressed her lack of self-confidence with this proposed action: To read a good book on building self-confidence by August 2nd and implement at least three ideas immediately upon finishing the book." She addressed increasing her assertiveness with a similar proposed action: "To read a good book on improving assertiveness by September 15th and to implement no less than three new ideas upon completing the book." She also included a proposed action involving getting certification as a project manager in the electrical contracting industry by a certain date.

When Jill re-took the MADI after six coaching sessions, her co-workers rated her significantly higher on self-confidence and assertiveness than they had originally. The President of the company also indicated that she was considerably more effective in dealing with clients after completing her coaching sessions.

One final example of successful coaching was Peter. Peter was the Chief Operating Officer of a region in a banking organization. In determining his key developmental needs, one of Peter's most significant failings was trying to do everything himself. Peter dealt with his poor delegation skills by coming up with the following proposed action: "To make a desk card that says, 'Can someone else do this?' and to implement this idea immediately."

When Peter was evaluated by his co-workers after completing the six coaching sessions, he was rated significantly higher on delegation than he had been originally. His proposed action was very simple, but it obviously was extremely effective in getting him to change his behavior.

An example of unsuccessful coaching
Unfortunately, coaching does not always work. It cannot be successful when someone does not buy into the concept and does not want to change his behavior.

Salvatore was a person who would not benefit from coaching. When we met initially to discuss the process, he said, "This is a bunch of garbage, I don't believe in it, and I refuse to participate in the coaching program." Obviously, Salvatore, a sales executive, was not going to benefit from coaching because he refused to even try it.

Another model/approach to coaching
My approach to coaching is not the only on that works. One other consultant whom I saw at a conference used a model that was extremely effective. He worked exclusively with CEO's and he talked to them on the phone daily for one year after determining their key developmental needs. He also met with each CEO and his co-workers monthly and got feedback on progress or lack thereof.

This consultant charged an extremely high fee but he spent a lot of time on his process and obtained excellent results.

One could also design a process in between what I do and what the consultant described above does. For example, the coach could talk to the coachee weekly on the phone or via e-mail, meet with her and her co-workers every six weeks, and continue the process for six to nine months.

The key elements in coaching

Regardless of the approach one takes, one element of the process is essential: establishing trust and support with the client. If this does not exist, the coaching will not be successful. If, on the other hand, the coach is able to get the coachee to trust him and believe he is out for the coachee's best interests, the process can be very successful. This is true even if the person being coached is initially opposed to the idea, such as Bob, whose case I discussed previously in this chapter.

I described above how an outside change agent can modify the behavior of someone who exhibits The Phenomenon. As I said earlier, a second condition that needs to be met in order for someone exhibiting TP to change is that a trusted person in the individual's life whom he cares about has to convince him that he is doing things that have an adverse effect on himself, the trusted associate, and others.

This is no easy task, as you might imagine. Obviously, before the trusted person can convince the individual he needs to change, the trusted person has to recognize the adverse behaviors the individual is exhibiting. An instrument such as the one in the Appendix can help the trusted person identify that the individual does, in fact, exhibit various behavior associated with TP. After this occurs, a significant challenge faces the trusted person: convincing her significant other, long-term friend, or close working associate that he is hurting himself, the trusted person, and various others with some of his behavior.

For some people exhibiting characteristics of The Phenomenon, just having a trusted person tell him that she is being hurt by his behavior might be enough to convince him of the need to change. Unfortunately, for some people showing signs of TP, the trusted person might need to threaten leaving the individual if he does not attempt to change some of his behavior. Possibly losing a spouse, significant other, long-term friend or close working associate might be sufficient motivation to convince some of those exhibiting TP to try to change.

Despite having sufficient motivation to try to change, and having a qualified change agent to assist in the process, not everyone will be capable of modifying his behavior to an appreciable extent. Nonetheless, it is always worth the effort to _try_ to make significant changes.

CHAPTER 6

WHAT CAN PEOPLE DO WHO HAVE A BOSS OR OTHER CO-WORKER EXHIBITING THE PHENOMENON?

Some possible ways to deal with your boss

If you have a supervisor who exhibits The Phenomenon, she can make your life a living hell. Many people in this situation might say something like: "Life is too short to put up with this!"

One option is to leave the position and transfer somewhere else in the organization. This alternative can be a very good one for some people. A possible drawback, however, can be that some individuals showing signs of The Phenomenon can be very vindictive. They might view someone's transfer as a personal affront to them and might decide to try to hurt the transferred person's reputation and career.

Many individuals, especially those further up in the organizational hierarchy, may not have the option of transferring to another position in their organization. Some of these people may choose another alternative: leaving the firm. Once again, however, a vindictive boss might try to "poison the water" regarding the departing person in terms of a poor performance evaluation. This negative reference might deter potential employers from hiring the individual wanting to leave.

Some people will manage to secure another position, however, even though their supervisor may provide a negative performance evaluation to the supervisor in the new organization. Of course, if a person has a supervisor who exhibits signs of The Phenomenon and may be vindictive, she probably would not use that boss as a reference. Nonetheless, many employers want to talk to the former supervisor, even if the potential employee would not want them to do so.

Many people having a supervisor showing signs of TP would not want to leave their position or organization. What can these people do?

One possible option is to confront the supervisor and talk about how his behavior is adversely affecting the employee. It is possible that this might have an impact on the boss and get him to modify his behavior is some ways. This is most likely to occur if the staff member uses what is called an 'I message': "When you do _____, it makes me feel _____". This is much better than a 'You message': "You always _____", or "You never _____." The effect of 'You messages' is invariably defensiveness, anger, or a counterattack.

On the other hand, 'I messages' focus on how the behavior makes the staff member <u>feel.</u> It is difficult to argue that someone does not <u>feel</u> a certain way.

Some individuals might want to confront a boss exhibiting signs of The Phenomenon but they tend to shy away from any type of confrontation with anyone. These individuals might consider assertiveness training. There are many courses available throughout the U.S. on how to be more assertive. Taking such a course might serve to give an individual the courage to confront his supervisor and give him some tools to deliver his message as well. Unfortunately, however, regardless of the approach used, the typical individual showing signs of The Phenomenon feels that he can do no wrong. As a result, he is most likely to react to any criticism, regardless of how is it presented, in a negative manner. This could involve anger, vindictiveness, or denial, asserting that the staff member is the one who has a problem, not him. This might result in negative future performance evaluations, reduced future salary increases, no pay increases, demotion, or even firing.

As I indicated in Chapter V, in many cases the only approach likely to change the behavior of someone exhibiting The Phenomenon is one involving a trusted person whose opinion the one showing signs of TP values. This valued person has to try to convince the individual that he needs to change some of his behavior. In order to be able to effect that change, a qualified, experienced coach has to work with the individual to try to assist him in making changes.

Some possible ways to deal with yourself

One way for someone to deal with a co-worker exhibiting The Phenomenon is to take a course in meditation. Having such a co-worker is obviously extremely stressful. Meditation is an excellent means for dealing with stress.

In an article from Psychology Today by Cory Barbor originally published on May 1, 2001, the author said the following: "Recent research indicates that meditating brings about dramatic effects in as little as a ten minute session. Several studies have demonstrated that subjects who meditated for a short time showed increased alpha waves (the relaxed brain waves) and decreased anxiety and depression."

The author went on to say the following: "The physical art of meditation generally consists of simply sitting quietly, focusing on one's breath, a word or phrase."

There are many courses on meditation offered regularly by qualified people throughout the country. Checking the internet is an easy way to identify an appropriate course offered near you.

Another way to deal with a co-worker exhibiting the Phenomenon is to take a course in mindfulness. It is one type of meditation that has become increasingly popular in recent years. According to John Kabat-Zinn, one of the pioneers in the field: "Mindfulness is awareness, cultivated by paying attention in a sustained and particular way in which we engage in 1) systematically regulating our attention and energy; 2) thereby influencing and possibly transforming the quality of our experience; 3) in the service of realizing the full range of our humanity; and 4) our relationships with others and the world". (The quote is from Mindfulness for Beginners, p. 1, published by Sounds True, Inc. in 2012.)

Like other meditation-based courses, ones in mindfulness are offered throughout the country regularly by qualified personnel. You can check the internet to find such a course being offered in a location near you.

Another way to deal with yourself if you have a co-worker who shows signs of TP is to become involved in coaching. Work-related coaching is a one-on-one process in which you learn more effective ways to do your job. This includes dealing with co-workers.

I described my approach to coaching in Chapter V. Coaching has become increasingly popular in recent years (I have been doing it for over forty years, long before it was popular). Checking the internet will provide names of various coaches in your area. However, I have one caveat: Make sure the coach you decide on is a truly qualified professional.

Since coaching has become more popular in recent years, it has unfortunately attracted many unqualified people who call themselves "coaches". A qualified coach is a psychologist or other professional who has had many years of relevant advanced education, training and experience. Unfortunately, a high school graduate who took a course in coaching and who is 19 years old can call himself "a coach". I would not.

Another possible way to help yourself deal with someone who exhibits signs of The Phenomenon is to become involved in counseling. Counseling is different from work-related coaching in that it typically first involves diagnoses via the Diagnostic and Statistical Manual of Mental Disorders – 5 (DSM-5), published by the American Psychiatric Association in 2015; coaching does not.

There are many types of counseling. Qualified counselors are psychologists, psychiatrists, psychotherapists, or other mental health professionals licensed by state boards. They have advanced degrees: at least a master's degree in a relevant field, a Ph.D. or an M.D. Ideally, they have many years of relevant, successful experience. Checking the internet may be a first step in finding a qualified counselor. Word of mouth is another means of finding a good one near you.

Another way to help yourself in dealing with someone exhibiting symptoms of The I Know Everything About Everything Phenomenon is to read a relevant self-help book. There are many good books on meditation and mindfulness which can be very helpful, such as one mentioned previously by John Kabat-Zinn, Mindfulness for Beginners. Many good relevant CD's are also available. Checking Amazon.com or other resources on the internet can provide the information you seek.

CHAPTER 7

WHAT IS THE FUTURE FOR THOSE EXHIBITING SYMPTOMS OF THE PHENOMENON AND THE PEOPLE AROUND THEM?

People who recognize the need for change

Few, if any, people who exhibit signs of The Phenomenon are likely to change their behavior solely on their own. As I said in Chapter V, to make behavior change likely, someone close to the individual exhibiting TP, whose opinion he respects, needs to be involved. This could be a spouse, significant other, close friend, or a long-time work associate.

Also, as I indicated in Chapter V, an additional person needs to be involved to make behavior change likely: a highly qualified, experienced coach. Ideally, this would be a business psychologist or another individual who has a successful track record of prompting behavior change.

If the two individuals mentioned above are involved, and the person needing to change his behavior is highly motivated to do so, there is a fairly high probability that modification of his actions will occur.

In what ways is the behavior of the person likely to change? If she is a CEO or other executive, her management style may change dramatically. For example, she may demonstrate considerably more empathy than previously. She may begin to make substantial efforts to try to see situations from others' point of view. She might also start to listen to, and heed advice from, staff members. In addition, she might demonstrate more concern for employees' welfare. Also, she might no longer act as if she were "special" and that rules and laws do not apply to her.

If the person exhibiting signs of TP is a professional, such as an attorney, he might begin to acknowledge that he sometimes makes mistakes. Also, he might admit that he does not know everything there is to know about the law. In addition, he might acknowledge that he is not an expert in all facets of life (e.g., religion, politics, art, music, etc.).

If the person in question were another type of professional, say a physician, he might no longer brag that everything good that happens is solely a result of his talents and expertise. In addition, he might stop taking advantage of others for his personal gain.

So far, I have mentioned ways in which someone exhibiting The Phenomenon might change his behavior for the better and become a more effective executive or professional. What about how others might be affected by such behavior change?

If the individual who changed were an executive, her staff members might be more receptive to the modification in management style and be more receptive to continuing to work for her. If the individual were a spouse of the person enacting positive behavioral change, she might feel that the relationship is much better and that she would want to continue as the marital partner.

If the person who demonstrated change had a close friend, the person might find the friendship to be significantly better than in the past. The friend might also seek out the changed individual for other activities to be shared.

What about the impact of changed behavior on a significant other? I believe that this person might find the changed individual to be a good candidate for a more in-depth relationship, such as marriage.

Another issue to be considered is the impact on society of favorable changes in individuals demonstrating characteristics of The Phenomenon. I think that if a substantial number of people were able to change in various ways, this could have a major societal impact. For example, many spouses, significant others, close friends, and close work associates of those exhibiting The Phenomenon would be much happier in general and more effective in their jobs. This could affect society very favorably. It could result in greater job productivity and increased satisfaction with life in general.

People who do not recognize the need for change

What about people demonstrating The Phenomenon who do not recognize the need to change their behavior? I believe it is likely that such individuals would continue to have limited effectiveness in their jobs. This would result from their continuing to exhibit the following adverse behaviors:

- Failing to admit mistakes.
- Believing that rules and laws do not apply to them.
- Believing that they know everything about their field of expertise.

- Believing that they know everything about all aspects of life.
- Bragging that everything favorable that happens occurs because of their brilliance and superior talents.
- Taking advantage of others for personal gain.
- Failing to show empathy for others.
- Lacking concern for the welfare of others.
- Failing to listen to the advice of people who are knowledgeable and experienced.

The likely impact on those individuals surrounding people who exhibit signs of The Phenomenon, should they fail to see a need to change their behavior, is that the associates would continue to feel very frustrated, unappreciated, underutilized, and angry.

Having many people feel unappreciated, frustrated, underutilized, and angry is likely to have a significant adverse impact on society in general.

Further research needed

As was mentioned earlier in this book, The I Know Everything About Everything Phenomenon is a new concept which I identified. As is true for all new concepts, further research needs to be done on all facets of it. Specifically, additional research should be done on what it is. My definition of The Phenomenon should be reviewed and corroborated by others.

Also, as I indicated earlier in the book, I believe that The Phenomenon is caused primarily by someone experiencing continued success. Further study should be done on my postulated cause to determine whether this is valid.

In addition, in the Appendix I indicated how The Phenomenon can be measured. Additional research should be done on my criteria to ensure they are appropriate.

Additional study also needs to be done regarding how The Phenomenon can be changed. As I indicated, I believe that in order for someone to change his behavior, he needs to: 1) be highly motivated; 2) have someone close to him want him to modify his behavior, and 3) have an experienced coach with a successful track record work with him. These items need to be studied further to determine whether they are the appropriate criteria and whether additional factors need to be involved in order to effect successful behavioral change.

Finally, additional research should be done concerning how a person best deals with someone who exhibits The Phenomenon. I indicated a number of ways this can be done; these need to be validated and it needs to be determined whether other ways would also be useful.

Inventory to Identify People Who Exhibit The I Know Everything About Everything Phenomenon

Directions: Rate the person 1-5 by circling the appropriate number according to the behavior exhibited in each item.

Scoring will be explained later.

1. Believes he/she knows everything about his/her field.	1 Believes he knows very little about his field	2 Believes she has a lot to learn about her field	3 Believes he is somewhat knowledgeable about his field	4 Believes she is an "expert" about her field	5 Believes he knows all there is to know about his field
2. Believes he/she is omniscient (i.e., knows everything about every aspect of life).	1 Believes he knows little about most aspects of life (e.g. financial matters, politics, religion, etc.)	2 Believes she has a lot to learn about most aspects of life	3 Believes he is somewhat knowledgeable about most aspects of life	4 Believes she is an "expert" on virtually every subject	5 Believes he knows all about virtually every subject
3. Refuses to admit his/her mistakes.	1 Is the first to admit his mistakes	2 Is somewhat reluctant to admit her errors	3 Will admit to making mistakes but justifies his behavior	4 Seldom will admit to making a mistake	5 Never admits he did something wrong
4. Loves to give advice without being asked.	1 Never gives advice about anything	2 Occasionally advises others on the action they should take	3 Sometimes advises others about what they should do	4 Frequently advises others about their impending action	5 Always tells others what they should do

	1	2	3	4	5
5. Loves to pontificate without being asked for his/her opinion.	Never lectures others	Occasionally lectures others on some subjects	Sometimes lectures others on some subjects	Frequently pontificates about some subjects	Frequently pontificates about virtually every subject
6. Refuses to listen to others for advice.	Always gives consideration to others' advice	Frequently listens to others' advice	Sometimes does not seriously consider others' opinions	Seldom gives much credence to others' advice	Never follows the advice of anyone else
7. Believes he/she is "special".	Never expects special consideration	Seldom expects special consideration	Sometimes expresses the belief that she is "special"	Often indicates that he has "special" status	Virtually always lets others know that she is "special"
8. Feels the rules and/or laws do not apply to him/her.	Always obeys the rules and laws	Frequently follows usual customs and obeys laws	Sometimes follows customary practices and obeys laws	Often does not follow usual customs and/or obey laws	Feels the customary rules and laws do not apply to her
9. Feels he/she is "better" than others.	Always says she is equal to others	Frequently says he is equal to others	Sometimes acts as if she is "better" than others	Often acts as if he is "better" than other people	Always acts as if she is superior to everyone else
10. Makes up his/her mind before hearing all of the facts.	Always listens to what others have to say before making up his mind	Frequently listens to what others have to say before making up her mind	Sometimes listens to others' information before making a decision	Frequently makes up her mind before hearing all of the facts	Virtually always makes up his mind before hearing all of the facts
11. Lacks empathy.	Is extremely adept at empathizing with others	Is very good at empathizing with others	Has adequate empathy	Has limited empathy	Is totally lacking in empathy

	1	2	3	4	5
12. Fails to demonstrate concern for others.	Always expresses concern for other people	Frequently expresses concern for others	Sometimes expresses concern for others	Seldom shows concern for others	Almost never demonstrates concern for others
13. Takes advantage of others for his/her gain.	Never takes advantage of other people	Occasionally takes advantage of others for her gain	Sometimes takes advantage of others	Often takes advantage of others	Nearly always takes advantage of others for her gain
14. Has a sense of entitlement.	Never feels that he is entitled to anything more than others	Occasionally demonstrates a sense of entitlement	Sometimes demonstrates a sense of entitlement	Often shows a sense of entitlement	Always demonstrates a sense of entitlement
15. Feels that everything good that happens to him/her is due to his/her brilliance and talents.	Always feels he is lucky when something good happens	Frequently feels he is lucky when something good happens	Sometimes says he is lucky when something good happens	Often believes that his good fortune is due to his brilliance or talents	Virtually always believes that his good fortune is due to his efforts alone
16. Loves to brag about his/her accomplishments and talents.	Never brags about her talents or accomplishments	Occasionally brags	Sometimes brags	Often brags about her accomplishments or talents	Is always bragging about what she has done or her talents

Scoring: Add up the total score for this person.

70-80   It is extremely likely that this person exhibits The I Know Everything About Everything Phenomenon.

60-69   It is somewhat likely that this person demonstrates The Phenomenon (TP).

45-59   This person may exhibit TP.

32-44   This person probably does not demonstrate TP.

31 and below   This individual does not exhibit The Phenomenon.

ABOUT THE AUTHOR

D oug Soat is a Consulting Psychologist who works with busi-
nesses and other organizations. He does employee selection and coaching and has had over 43 years of successful
experience in these areas in the U.S., the U.K., and Australia.
Also, for the past 24 years he has done psychological evaluations
of people with disabilities for the State of Wisconsin.

He received his B.A. in psychology from Cornell University in
1969. He got his M.S. in clinical psychology and Ph.D. in educational psychology (with an emphasis in counseling) in 1974. In
1981 he received his M.B.A. in management from the University
of Wisconsin-Whitewater.

Dr. Soat has been a licensed psychologist in the state of
Wisconsin since 1980.

He has been married for over 44 years to Lynn and he has two
sons, two daughters-in-law, and four granddaughters.

www.ingramcontent.com/pod-product-compliance
Lightning Source LLC
Chambersburg PA
CBHW050553280326
41933CB00011B/1830

* 9 7 8 0 9 9 8 8 6 8 1 1 0 *